Lances
All
Alike

Suzanne
Zelazo

Lances
All
Alike

Coach House Books, Toronto

first edition

 Canada Council   Conseil des Arts
for the Arts   du Canada

 ONTARIO ARTS COUNCIL
CONSEIL DES ARTS DE L'ONTARIO
an Ontario government agency
un organisme du gouvernement de l'Ontario

Canadä

Published with the generous assistance of the Canada Council for
the Arts and the Ontario Arts Council. Coach House Books also
acknowledges the support of the Government of Canada through
the Canada Book Fund and the Government of Ontario through
the Ontario Book Publishing Tax Credit.

LIBRARY AND ARCHIVES CANADA CATALOGUING IN PUBLICATION

Zelazo, Suzanne, author
        Lances all alike / Suzanne Zelazo.

Poems.
Issued in print and electronic formats.
ISBN 978-1-55245-362-9 (softcover).
        I. Title.

PS8599.E395L36 2018   C811'.6   C2018-900933-0
                                               C2018-900934-9

Lances All Alike is available as an ebook: ISBN 978 1 77056 534 0
(EPUB), ISBN 978 1 77056 537 1 (PDF)

Purchase of the print version of this book entitles you to a free
digital copy. To claim your ebook of this title, please email
sales@chbooks.com with proof of purchase. (Coach House Books
reserves the right to terminate the free digital download offer at
any time.)

'... are they weapons or scalpels?
            Whetted to brilliance
                by the hard majesty of that sophistication which is
        superior to opportunity,
these things are rich instruments with which to experiment.'

                            — Marianne Moore, 'Those Various Scalpels'

EXCISION I

The Bisected Poems of
Mina Loy and Baroness Elsa

'Widows in Greenwich Village'

Kissing—a—lap—yelping noise
white flesh quakes
morning—in—hallway

Lethargic ecstasy of steps
jazz—stutters maiden saplings
penetrate
—spiritual—tinkling
high-strung ukulele
groves of grace

Electric crown crashes
through shampooed sound

Colossal absentee
black-blue
through starvation streets
incurves

Salacious survivor dragging
kitchen stove bathtub

Husband—
how secretly you
flutter
conjure
modulate

This anemic devotion
unfurled and leaning
tropic and readymade

Trailing the Moon Over Kentucky
(To Djuna from the Two of Us)

Stuffed maze—Moreover

the moon— — —
night pitched face to the skies
intricate ménage

Fluorescent pillar
mould-steeped air—

Corpse silver—circular
spellcast
looms dense and touching panic
clogged beat
of eardrum—
thermal icicles
coercive as coma
maniacal river uplaughs—
frail as this blooming

Arabesque of Victory
(an omen)

Women or widows within uniform
—honeysuckle fists

Lapping tears sweep
blue
discover blossom fire
under shady tree
grotesque
dove's feather
drumming
sugar lake
the cargo of our dissonance

Ohio—Crab-Angel Carousel

Atomic sprite
perched to the west
monster stallion
on—river—reeds
poplars
revolving

Circus sun's caress
something the contour
of captured crab's
pearly claws

Performance becomes her—
juxtaposed hemispheres
form a squat concubine
azure and fervid

Baroque calf *en pointe*
—cosmic ballerina
in effigy

Chrysanthemum angler—
brain sugar of sweet
rose-flecked
ebony cloud
—gibes
its manly legs
masquerade of
rainbow ice
bite this tempest

Startled
orchestra
crab-crashes
to silence

Sediment of summer

Pity My Potency

I enter the
contraction—

A circle
in every direction

Congested cosmos

Prolonged Priestess of Intention
nerve-scraped
electric pain—
delirium's
distorted mountain

Sell her ink
exotic actors
in vacuum interlude
giving life its feathered apology
precipitating into glory
pure
this was—is—ever—shall—be

Blurring
stretched muscle
—hushed halo
ludicrous climax

City Stir on Third

I

Dancewind disappear
bronze careening

Shadow bodies
flower-stained
with swish—

Tree arms of neon signs
lips ablaze
hueless
contorted tailor

Moon riding
eerie's undress
tongue touch
—whirlpool on eardrum—

II

Flower-soaked city
compensating
seafaring jewellery
—electric poverty

Appalling sister
dumped in a chimney
sugar-coated goddess
meet
another's soot heart
her lovely feet
shell-centred
in their sentence
illumined strangely
with mirage

Tendered Buttons

Red spoon
of the laboratory
brimming sea whispers— — —

Crushed moon
sinuous consciousness
congealed fantasia

Ribald tonnage
radium swoon

Brancusi's Golden Equinox

Harpsichord
become aesthetic archetype
patient howl—
metallic peasant God

Naked growl of ivory
furred rhythm
unwinged cannon step—

Lopped form
nuclear wind
inflated crest
the absolute act

Hurtling clouds
incandescent curve
moonstruck breast

Membrane—licked nights— — —
split gong on polished brain
bird shrills

'Cut Piece': Mina and Elsa at the Arensbergs'

— — —   — — —
— — — — — — — — — — —

— —

— — — — —   — — — — —
— — —

—
—
—
—
—
—
— — — — — — — — —   —

—
—   —
— — — — — — — — — — —
            — — —

            — — —

— — — — — — — —   — — — !
— — —
            — — — —

— — — — — — — — — — —

            — — — — —

            —

            —

Manière de Passer à l'Autre

Life in Florence
a hat
defines her death

Lola her love
pens possession
rules space time
only tenses tame measure
immense echo

Ménage à Cinq

Mistress of East Eleventh
ventriloquized her generation

Hidden wrinkle
of a century
guidebook avatar
scalpels so beautiful
she found
diction posturing
Trojan self-hypnotism

Expediency
denied metre
lexical habitat
of broken grammar

Deviant daughter dressed
lampshading
curious disciples

Mocking
lunar cannon
possessed of valance
desired ghosts
tumbling

The Blind Man
inebriate dancer
sanctions bowery vision
seances from trash

Window-Dressing Virgin

Marble city presses the door's chain
netted virgins on plumb streets
their hats are not ours
amethyst cap confessional
rainsteep—nightdresses squeak

Pearl skies wasting their giggles
no dots stand
wince-whip with soft wings
circus city conjuring

White virgins for sale
our windows sing for men
hush-tinged
the city deep throbs
cleaving stars

The Insipid Ride of Melsina: A Narrative

The door was hole-proof— —

Melsina—God knows
spread thickly— —
her thighs a scarlet afternoon

Corporeally—transcendentally—consecutively
until skin is two windows if necessary
don't rush sloping lines

Happy women shape
palpable fantasy on Sundays

Patience Melsina— —
being female jars subjoy
always sanitary

Flowered soul poetry
composite effigy
crinoline
ready-to-wear
you'll feel outside time
and woollen
a dish of his ego
can kill

Paris and garters—madam—
succulent and unlawful
and cellophane
—will you try it—
love kisses
exact flavour—an occasional caress

His mind
fearing lighted wheels and axles
—might blind her

Weeping willow watching from window
fallen stars

Jelly rub—
—a red flannel poem
Melsina wanted
electro-pneumatic aspirations
devotional
monogamy remained the axis

Don't learn by heart
the grandest thing—no boiling required—
oh life!

Smell original sunshine
children in rapid transit— —
where circles hesitate
having no vices
only
chocolatey narrative and that house

Lunar Lorr!

Cosmic cocaine miracle—
silver fixed somnambulists

Cornucopia of thighs

Nocturnal Cyclops
watch shattered glass
concubine moon maintenance

Flux-driven draperies
hallucinatory atom
oval logic
fascinated flight

Hanging off shutters
—Luxembourg gardens
morning light on high-waisted nuns

*

Silence of hands touching hands
she asphyxiates on discretion
measures the floor with her surplus

Invisible antique shield
breasts that detonate and plenty
flicker of tongue—a practical daughter

Springs scuttling goldenseal
flippant changeling—she towers

Twenty-six miles of sinew—
a gesture to puddles and stars
murmur like another kind of shatter
melancholic and lamenting
sweet chaos of stillness

—She is brandy-lipped and mooning—
water for swallows and sapphire

Congruent

Cortical velvet mouthbloom
aloof on syncopated sunshine
bruised passage of limelight

Agape under Northern Lights

Daughters of deco
echo of sunshine
forever and always and sometimes

EXCISION 2

Engendering Exiles

'[*Exiles*] won't do for the stage … I don't believe an audience could follow it… '

— Ezra Pound to James Joyce, 1915

Citable Gestures

I

The window, Dublin, further back,
framed panels leading forward,
the window, green plush sunlight—
portfolio-shaped mistress arrived
nervously down there, rather wet.

His study can wait, wearing a letterbox,
Justice blushing,
her hands, Italian folding doors,
sad sketches slightly written.
His elbows, his knees, his hands
you would find sometimes cruel.

Shyly my mind attracts you.
My book published,
again,
perhaps my brain
running
repeats uncertainty,
sinks confidence.
Feel my book
for nine long years,
my struggle for your eyes,
silent scorn.

Your soul bends,
crosses to the lounge.

*

I felt your secret garden, your garter, a kiss.
Your going changed everything.

Pale repressed energy.
Peace exists somewhere,
freely, wholly,
terribly hard
for my dead mother.

She rises,
bidding a break with the past.

His forehead in exile
understanding tongues.

*

A stone evening, a lavender dress

found here shaking—
tragic movements,
for a private compromise.
Harmonic hesitation
in his hands.

Nine years came back to me
tired and dirty—
night impression.
Knitting ladies speak.

I know your eyes,
my house breaks.
Listening lips will wait.

He read your book in Dublin.
Public past is impulsive,
hanging language
on sensations.
Mysterious young articles,
your future played to wait
in our house,
his glass revelry musing
blasphemy.
The women have two keys
for all occasions.

Everything can be
polished against lips,
bird pressing stone.

Paperweight pause.

Think here among people,
collect a hundred years
without rising.
Come home.
A descendant
shaking candidly
with a gesture of milk.

Robbers in the garden
sink swiftly,
fingering the roses absently.
The moon,
crumpling kisses with a shrug.

Dreadfully jealous, the slip
of paper reads her.
The couch stares, remembers
a curious, bounding liar.

Mother rambles except to you,
violently then and now.
Liberty is to write,
to believe
a gesture between love.

Following false throws,
for years I came back.

Diseased words remember,
Yes, she says, *yes*.

II

Piano music draped yellow across the bars
he inhales, an umbrella was too much blood.

Wondering suspicious,
she could break everything,
rapidly,
the word you never dared say.

Wooing, watching you watching me, a tortured
happening without roses, thieves glancing until
love would go so boldly.

Dear fervent gesture,
I will take language by violence,
forget rights,
claim nothing,
a luminous certitude.

Now away alone, my conscience told me nothing.
Angel union, warped waiting, my mind paces and leans
against our hearts, against the book.

Neglecting forms.
Her body
poorer in love.
The past is breathless,
is now our noble gaze,
a spectre of passion.

Escape language roused in my brain,
mastering your part,

a knock to appeal,
Question the porch.

Waterproof Ireland.
You knew jealous men
hate helplessly with violence.

Here, her eyes remain hidden.
Opportunity unpins respect,
the name I trusted to delight my soul.
Wisdom will remain.

A little garden
clasping defiantly a word,
an experiment
with polite hand,
drawing distressed rain.

Truth can be sweet, velvet secrets flicker over
his shoulder toying with revenge.

Her wind enters,
the sound of rising
detained light, wrong now
knowing his gift,
never three
together unheeding,
bending the boat away.

You chose books I wrote.
Nine years more strange.
Lamp leaps,
caressing truth.

III

Her delighted legs spinning Ireland,
devilment for tea, a kettle crossing.

Folded between curtains,
knotted hands about to halt,
dreamrain knocks her chair.
Somewhere curious books remember.

Wide bookshelves extinguished
her cracking.
Clean embrasure.
Halting, she listens.
A knock of doubt,
fingers on the middle hour,
warmly watching her paper.
Yesterday a noise,
sinking valise quarrel.

Smoothing the movement,
my conscience brought back Ireland.

Your letters blushing suddenly.
She rises,
writing to feel this house,
to hate the past truly,
to hate that he writes
in wonder.

The door bends the garden.
Full of voices I could not see.
Stammering to forget,

contorting the marriage like a promise,
vital victory.

Spiritual decade of fierce eyes.
The doorway dawned
in her hour of need,
a man under the rest.

Accuse long eyelashes,
send a message,
try through different churches.
Press paper moments
till his study left me, what I am.

False listening,
she nods.
Every dead mother turns.

Tears covering her shoulder.
A stranger
dressed quietly in brown,
coming toward my mind,
wandering in my image.

The table points to her foreign parts,
country silence.

Fresh herring on the chair,
that is truth.

Your friend buries his face
in Dublin Bay.

Her Donnybrook death,
I walked all stained
with my valise,
my story is yours now.

I wrote all night,
full of voices
flattened at the window.

In exile
wherever you go.
Excitable hands,
and his dressing gown.

He went away, left epigrams
that looked like women.

Morning drove his hunger.
Meeting
the roof, the city, the river
ended at the sky.

Everything rises,
earnestly a dream, a softer real,
an alarmed goodbye.

EXCISION 3

Sutured Portraits

Needlepoint

In the flesh
we are a century of catastrophic echoes,
a riot of stones
hurled against the afterglow.

Simmer of bone on bone,
missiles unfurled,
rapture on our lips
where the sutures were.

Sins of Splendor

Three Marys, one for each framed stagger.
Limestone statues in their honour
erected in basements.
They know about consumption.
They buy into dissonance
split three ways.

They are powder blue and unapologetic.
Together they follow the hound,
rooting prismatic,
shedding the century,
they turn uranium skyward,
unplug orchid bulbs and laughter.

Three Marys of the East and West,
sea-brine mothers
shrinking driftwood and glass.
They stroke the hound,
flowering its paws
of cranberry sunset and iron.

Vanished at the equator,
they have come back,
dreamt about Atlantis
on the shores off Nauset.
Hollow hemisphere,
the hound leapt over,
Sylvian Fissure.

Tender hesitation of whimsy.
Wheat gatherers and sonnet makers,
less easy than mink or wool
in the turret, after an evening
above the breathline.
The hound lets the Marys pass,
where coral and shellfish
leave us skeptical.

Three Marys splintered and resurging where
amethyst is Grecian.
Urns meant for hounding—
the afternoon spent basking.
Hind legs curled under belly,
sweet hollow of a canine roar.
Heap of bones in hexameter.

Blue Notes

I

I spill my centre into yours.

There's nothing more beautiful
than your eyes closing over our uprising,
finger raised in silence
complicit in the resonance.
Celestial binding,
follow the lunar lining
of the fullness between us.

Intimate crimson peak,
vintage celestial.
These frozen rites homespun,
and embalmed.
Your gift, corrosive in the sun.
Our gifts, flippant and gorgeous with pallor.

II

Concussive
prowling of sinew and bone,
flesh notes in the cooling.

Pooled by the silence of your echo,
an impulse toward drowning.

Ours for the taking, not *un*making.

Atomic sky turns thick blister of flight.
Sibilant cadence of objection.

This stark minute undoes you.
Soon the sting will sting less,
mouthful of creasing and rage,
scurry the pedestal I stand on.

My wings,
thick petals and backbone,
fold to meet you.

Yet I am waiting,
less through vanishing than through interval.
Groping the rational toward a centre.

III

Acoustic single-sided love affair.
Scoop the clouds in an embrace.
Yet it's yours I want, not the clouds,
not their indiscriminate longing.
We are that we are,
the two of us.

Nightfall surprised us both.
A botched and myriad encounter.
Shrink the narrative,
let it pass.
Illuminate the bias.

Select the freefall.
Turn the haze electric,
we stumble less now,
having found the gesture.
Hands fussed,
our bodies bent with accent.

IV

Breathing the floodlight of moon,
iron fisted and threadbare.
The gills of this frayed flag
surrender.

Dismembered chasm of words,
this bliss of reciprocity.
Crystal refraction mollified,
shattered by the language of mining.

Her eyes heard it all,
cloaked in blue,
ribbons of jazz set her bones,
her scars a honeycomb craving.

Cher Ubu
(with love)

Beloved bachelor
stripped bare of his brides,
sonorous dusk laugh
caught in fractal ease.

Automatic canon kiss
where sad gems sigh.

Beneath conquest poems
pipelines sunsquinting.

Beep-bopping firefly
becoming a peerless flaw,
polished links of Lego.

Precocious echo.

His tongue in chenille chemise,
hands on buttercup shoulders,
dreaming of octopus girls and ambush.

Weeping Willow

Rain,
and even more,
the crushing of a slow refrain.

Celestial mime
to insinuate
the movement your hands make.

Sutures on a wet blank continuum.

Concussed

Here, the thinking is decorative, breathing out of range in myth. She is the deep blue quiver of its aftermath. Balance the ledger, tally the debt, it's strobe-lit and coupled. He slips like her hand through a paper mantel, foresees its various symbols. The swerve of too-narrow wrists. Small alcove of sleep where his grace uncoils and her skull cracks golden fever. Reluctant mother tongue, electric. She knew the bruised lilacs on his spine were from hiding—back up against the surge. She approximates the refill. Follows his hands in laying bricks, the perfect grammar of their fortress. Her trances are an affliction, a self-portrait and its silhouette. Shrink the cell, she warns. The flame in his throat, an eviction, a brimming meant for mining. Each morning blurs its translation. Here, she is the wet fold of drowning.

Punch Drunk

Wingtip against bone—distills her sprawl.

Each thought's an archive of your DNA,
the syntax of tiny, fragile words
fossil filaments of longing,
jagged synaptic gap.

And when you broke my jaw
I heard your heartstrings stir,
concentric ripple of the way you came,
finger raised in awe,
your body a crystalline moonglare,
its seismic slip inside me
a scream in reverse.

Poppies
rain-spotted and cruel
in the blinking
cathartic roar.

Spinning hydrogen atoms reel
unpillowed shooting stars.

Sound a wall,
music patched by colour transfer,
virtual choreography of tongues,
continuous shiver of wanting.

Your eyes too soft for torment,
so certain of shadows
and resurfacings.

Sandpaper neural grating,
phatic curvature of spine
adjacent to vision.

Your fist
multiple and fractal,
mine
a terrible pummel in real time.

Fly me over the reflex.

Sister Space

Sisters asleep at the fold,
while histories surface.
Sparrow-waisted, they hinge,
expose butterfly bruises.

Symmetrical, they shimmer
among gaps.
Double exposure of breastbone and fog.

Tufts of inflamed candour,
twinning the overlap.
With a feral flicker they swiften and billow.

Porcelain doubt,
an heirloom that devours
the space between them,
conjoined.

Swallowing sisters,
not fleeting, or shifting, or slaying,
but enjambing,
victorious.

Sundrift, Moonswell

I

Autumn, a war cry that summoned you
three miles of mud and resignation
to wade through, to unleash me.

A thousand frozen false reliefs,
the tangled history of strangers.

Aerial revision:

continuity of contradictions
in perfect connection.

Our eyes an artillery
we spoke through,
the shells at our feet,
an aria.

Collate this reading as writing,
always through the inner ear,
an idiom of incessant rising.

II

Downstream and wringing,
the storm at your throat.
forty proof and pounding,

When leaving gave sway,
we found wings for diving
where coolness enflamed us.

Three years a swelling sob.
A barbed-wire glare,
blond strangulation of ecstasy.
Concussive brotherhood of thunder.

Punctuate the embrace.
Metric rumble at your ankles,
seismic pummel of earthlight.

III

Our mothers mined ruined
line breaks in the naked sound of listening.

Burn me a river of song
in a mill town meant for silent winning streaks.
We followed a hankering moon
while the bed chimed,
my head in your lap.

Falling skyward
in the pond,
a frozen afterthought
where the fish
dream through.

IV

Double flight beneath my chair,
symbolic. In me you multiply
a million shards of two.
Tender strategy of skin,
sensorial tumble in space-time.

A lesson in counterpoint.
Ours is a windstorm meant to pacify,
a book made of flooding
and triumph,
calligraphic camouflage and meaning.

V

Supernova overload,
silk-screened serenade, the stirring.
Thursday morning clouds
bathing blissful, passage of flesh through slaughter.

Your lyric furnishings,
an art deco musing.
Futurist conqueror.
Curve of sycamore and cherrywood,
double-swing the shadow rising.

Coquettish cabinetry,
an alignment
concealing celestial stammer.

Ours is a milkglass enchantment
hanging electric quiver,
vertical regret,
a lacquered mirror of promise and abandon,
feathering,
when the winds change.

Under My Dress, A Thousand Startled Moons

Godfather of amputated limbs
aloof, afloat,
linguistic upswell.
Seizure poems of knotted glass,
cities to the left of leaving.

Concerning fusion
and circular recognition,
a shiver of abbreviated pleas.

He bribes interpretation,
braising lyrical assault.
Watermark or night stain
replacing fault lines with a clue.

Sault Ste. Marie,
her eyes, a runway union,
sepulchral syncopation,
she fumbles.

Parthenon of unfurled fists
thrash where the rapids flow.

Eccentric erasure,
tenuous passage of limelight,
divergent.
Deafening acoustic stare.

More awake than mistaken,
hemlines theatrical and slipping,
he rides the weather,
buoyant stagger on his lips.

Aphorisms of plenty
where his hands were.

Transference

Here's my bouquet
of virtual rain
near rock or doorframe.

Muted measure
hawksweep.

Spiral agent
listening.

A fleece, a bearer of shell-lined blows,
bind and unbind your Mayan mythos.

Couch-fissure,
passion surge.

I speak in curve of flutenote.
Leather and sinew contemplate
an arrow, a halo, a ghost bulb.

Projective Identification

Swift congress of chainmail,
an arrival.

Your books
on a gypsy caravan.
Fault lines seminal,
low ceiling crack,
your walls bloom.

Neon nerve cover.

Space articulates.
The comma I sit on
engulfs me,
honeysuckle prose,
tongue-tied and begging.

Your chair, obsessed with its frame,
imitates
oracular
youth.

The waiting room's a stammer.
Boulevard of crows
at my wrists,
an episode
of feeding
the glistening crossfire.

Tectonic Gaze

'So you have swept me back,'
slayed colour with your breath,
a nightsong,
a blighted tryst.

Embers over breasts
sampling my vista
wet with your sighs.

A kite,
hieroglyphic hostage,
remembers the slip.

Unfurl those golden fists,
a veil, a yolk, a swollen tragedy,
fleshquake in tender hesitation.

A glen as echo,
sinuous night,
The moon on my tongue
like your voice in my lap,
velvet whetted appetite.

Longing to collide,
hammer blow and orchid
hurling shadows where our flames were.
Language lifted in glass bouquets
hypnotic nectar cunning,
cocooning,
the way we once did.

Hivebound, the star explodes and your eyes
ash-whirl the protein altar
leaving codons of sonorous concordance
waving a startled rose to love.

Diviner

Deciduous trees leave
cracks in crystal canopies.
Splash pool, lucid
semiotic darkroom.

Kettle lake amnesia,
wake the Emperor not the Empress.

Rice paper bloats
the rhyme.

Retinal dream dislodged in the escarpment,
neural letterpress seduction
proper bound.

Headwater pearls
with angel rod and brushstroke.
Coded cataract occlusion,
ripple blow.
The bogs, a glass harmonica,
sing invisible faultlines.

Unfold the apple blossoms,
origami touch sound,
amplified amethyst kiss.

EXCISION 4

As I Lay Sighing

'It's like everything in the world for me is inside a tub full of guts, so that you wonder how there can be any room in it for anything else very important.'
— Dewey Dell

I: Fatherhood of Thieves

Glass eyes moving,
she can't wait.
        Barefooted aerialist
looked back,

her shame
poison again.

Looking lowered lightning,
unless a nipple and home,
pay enough to tell.

Precious little kept her eyes blank,
sometimes a man can't.

Devil take it here hissing,
no-sound echoes,
no-strings of sunset,
to lift tomorrow, intent and sad,
rubbing slow profile of sky.

Branch coiling
splints of time if you could
replace surges,
        pale moving hips.

Thought boiled the hem of her sleep,
she was close.
        Quiet her holes.

Sleep moonshines our legs,
nobody is water.

Swinging voice lashes,
fire sparks rain.
Planking fragments
whistling
the gap, my name.

I am a nimbus curtain,
            scorching crimson.

I went to find night,
on her back
swirling red barn.

Pieces of stars on his face.

Her lap flattens between road and bushes,
she cannot hear the undergrowth.

A hole to sound.
Body arched bushes,
carrying hills and stockings and cakes.

Red sand whisper,
hush entry.

White eyes and sudden
wagon whirls blind,
his jaw swings.

Nothing to send or set fire to,
watching the ground in starts.

Pure balance traded the burn,
  crossed her river hands,
  teaching shame.
Edges comfort the making.

Man-feel,
nine months of digging
born thinking.

It feels right to begrudge a space
watching music shovel sound.

One could see where music waited,
lazy walls for a spell.

Her face a queer window,
clawing,
scratching,
his back.

The ground laughing,
moved deliberate horror.

Springs ease spare legs,
cured wife.
Borrow a hole for giving nothing but
country looks.

Talcum powder burning,
striking cellar door.
The clock like a boy,
sitting on the curb.
She turned waiting,
box of light in her hands.

Home never a refuge.
Clock roosts in the trees
shining beyond bed.

Chalk-line pistols laughing,
seats of spy glass.

Money cakes
a lie,
touch package,
touch daughter,
thief on a shameful dare.

Seventeen years on loan
it's not I.
Father thief steals a minute
        whenever he wants.

Mail order this world,
        his world,
        his life,
        his teeth,
and all my gallant misses.

II: Dog's Eyes

Born a wife,
suddenly a mother.

Slip measure fixing
cotton mind.

Sing colour
to swell sky.

His hands,
a sad box of windows.

Air-shaped jewel,
I am too many shining thimbles
intent on tightening.

His chest a warm sinkhole.
Flesh turned laughing cold.
Back-flung willows
break the strain.

A promise of pistols blaze.

No word is open.
Standing now,
his promise
buried by the barn,
threatening
to come
as rain.

Cut speak.
Pay for squatting outrage.

I am come up hearing
wings of rain,
trading tomorrow for my name.

Wild womb outraged.
Empty gazing eyes,
my dress,

void hissing always
to feel I am
blowing silk hope.

Wheels of cotton sky
plowing pieces of you,
and I trace two ends,
sunk, shivering.

Tangle of eyes,
foam.

Jawing a word,
his wrists milking
what was hard.

Puzzle sleep,
an arc of shimmer.

Midnight lantern
would fumble in trying,
since leaves cannot usher.

Auctioned her ribs.
Forty acres of spring,
she cried,
her wet pretty back dancing up a jewel.
His lip tight to her flesh,
his eyes a mouthful of kill.
Ride that night in grass.

Find risk blaming him,
it lived under waiting,
under something like sense.
He held me,
I lay sighing.

Thick currents murmur.
Hell fire
begrudge mourning and counting.

Dimpled like undergrowth
musing,
suspended spectral voice.
I sit trembling,
blue like groaning.

Still he looks
floorless and free
like I will never be,
as if trading
trembling knees.

His expression
knew where speaking leans.

Lamplight from her lap
the trees beckon,
waving unbroken.

Arch-necked gaze,
slip into stream.

He lunges free and I
brace against rearing,
beyond the hammering
I jump.

Curl blandness
moulding home
here,
suspended and groping the bottom.

Shoulder the surface,
reading the shore
through his fingers.
Blue hands answer
the windows.

Nothing did not mean to kneel.
Secret thought,
whip flesh.
Afternoon hate,
bubbling.

I took him like a bird,
creaking slow curve of spring
going north, wild to Sunday,
driving strange like a house.

Quick clinging sounds,
I-not-I,
gaps like orphans.

Duty boiling because I utter,
sanctify the woods,
think shape.
Breast echo voiceless,
I wore sound
gone and over.

To kneel is just a matter of words.

Lips entered erring ashes,
I said grace.

Up to bed,
        lick his stomach,
        flap wet waiting,
        lifted and carried and stopped.

Undressing we drove
under rusted sheets of welcome.
The past flashes velvet.

Glass breeze blinking,
hung on nothing.

Yelling in the shade
something to spell
ten circles of sky.

Blame that minute on God and morning.

III: Split Land

Plumb centre turns precision
sunlit behind hips.

Cakes in summer break up thought,
breed good value.

Hot hands outdrawn,
cedar trees bend,
drunk metal.

Nothingness blowing my parts yonder.

Wet overalls
harness blue shadows,
shake my jewels,
slam empty reaches into chance.

He's knocking somewhere else,
like flowers nailing sleep.

Watch the corner,
the crest of him,
lighter in sun,
a bluff.

His hands collapse my weight.
Dry land borrows his mouth
where I keep cows.
The word,
dark like our wagon,
private
until rain upsets living.

Mother was partial to poison,
dying sometimes,
sawing yellow days full of holes.
Beyond the woods,
my sack for secret eyes
touching hands.

Helping words die without knowing,
the seam bevelled,
fixing new hope for women.
Blinking ahead,
her sweeping bed,
the cotton trimming
surprised and careful.

Second sight shutting down promise.
Bad luck like a woman
travelling to always,
moving to stay put.

A house because men in doorways
wanting,
when prowling,
charge me.

Heaven sending me
a luckless cyclone too late,
a bank of cinders.
Twenty-five pounds of giving
swapped clean off cloud breaks,
crooked bluff.

I am my mother uncoiling.
She is a sister storm,
weather-shaped brooding.
Her eyes clinging to
furious rooms,
the bed beginning to drain her,
listening to cessation.

Twilight, a composite face.
Her head sprawling in two frames,
the mattress expires.

Behind his mouth,
shattered mass of sky.

Sawdust sound
flung,
now fading.

Cut into pieces,
she did it.
Swooping twilight circus,
hands beneath dirt
to stall him,
crying through kicking.

Noise in dust on my shoulder.
Rolling heads
sometimes plunge
the air,
striking.

Whirling noise is green,
a deep cursing jewel.
Hope limps,
living sounds shaping,
I wonder.

Cut into ten days,
my guts are a country.

Rain pushes the lamplight,
kneeling.

Bluff nuzzle,
the air clumps,
tilted secret.
Moaning,
my body filled with wood.

Hush cow
disappearing slowly.
Nothing if moaning hips slope,
sheet-lightning.
Through my clothes,
I am blind earth.

A whirling crib shut around shadow,
bleeding glass.

Shadow-boxing a storm,
legs at last,
thumping the bed.
Lowering his knees,
hissing every minute.

Rain pulling
you.
Father's umbrella dripping
till dust fixing between us.

Feeble against sleep I am
empty,
unlamped,
no longer the shape
of home.

The water seams,
except a body is a hole made neater.

Notes

In a prescient essay on the artist Joseph Cornell (1903–72) and his assemblage boxes, Mina Loy considers artistic influence a form of collage: 'This appropriation of others' handiwork is not pilfering, but lifting out of the past another's sight tinged with family likeness – aspects added to the original by the altered observation of modern eyes.' This is the spirit in which I 'appropriate' the work of Loy and the Baroness, as well as that of Joyce and Faulkner. Specifically, the collection explores lines of influence and collaboration; I believe that when we read and write, we bring with us the imprint of everything that has ever moved us, thus we do so always as a collaboration.

The first sequence, 'The Bisected Poems of Mina Loy and Baroness Elsa,' stages an imaginary, collaged conversation between the modernist poet-painters and collagistes Mina Loy and Baroness Elsa von Freytag-Loringhoven who, in spite of numerous aesthetic resonances and common artist friends (notably, Djuna Barnes and Marcel Duchamp), never engaged with each other's work, collaborated, or visibly supported each other's practice. Imagining how they may have formed a partnership, I stitched snippets of sounds from the poems of Loy and the Baroness, braiding together their disparate lines where I saw them as lances very much alike.

The non-relationship of Loy and the Baroness figures as a curious 'absent presence' in modernist cultural history. This sequence also draws attention to the fact that despite their flamboyant personalities and contributions to modernism, the creative work of both women would end up being lost for decades. As artists, neither one was easily categorizable, and in fact their breadth, creative flexibility, and fluency among media are likely part of why early editors, publishers, and arbiters of taste derided or suppressed their work.

The title of this collection comes from Marianne Moore's 1917 poem 'Those Various Scalpels,' purported to be about Mina Loy and the poignant contrast between the artist's exceptional physical beauty and her exacting, perceptive, and acerbic language – seemingly incongruous with the image of a 'poetess' at the time.

Ezra Pound famously created the term 'logopoeia,' ('a dance of the intelligence among words and ideas and modification of ideas and characters') to describe the cerebral work of Mina Loy and Marianne Moore. The two were often likened, but Moore was never comfortable with this comparison. Nor with Loy's physicality.

I felt it was important to set these women alongside their male contemporaries whose work was recognized and esteemed even when it was difficult. To this aim, I include two other treated text sequences – a piece based on James Joyce's *Exiles* and the final section responding to William Faulkner's *As I Lay Dying* – that seek to solidify the female consciousness where masculine modernism has configured it as a resounding lack. In both, I trace through and tease out of the original texts my own reading, to which I add with my 'altered observation of modern eyes.'

Creating a kind of palimpsest through patterns of overwriting and excision, the complexities and subjectivity of Joyce's primary female character, Bertha, begin to emerge, and her presence in the play substantiates. Similarly, in writing through Faulkner's *As I Lay Dying*, I attempt to give Dewey Dell (Addie and Anse's only daughter) a depth, a more sustained and prominent subjectivity.

The middle section of poetic portraits of contemporary Canadian poets and artists honours to some extent the rich duality of poetry and painting both Loy and the Baroness pioneered. The collection is thus about the amplification of the female voice (both in the moment of artistic creation and in the future moments and voices it inspires). Where one voice begins and the other ends may be impossible to discern.

Bibliography

Faulkner, William. *As I Lay Dying: The Corrected Text.* New York: Vintage, 1987.

H.D. *Selected Poems.* Ed. Louis L. Martz. New York: New Directions, 1988.

Joyce, James. *Exiles.* New York: Dover, 2002.

———. *Letters of James Joyce.* Volume II. Edited by Richard Ellmann, London: Faber and Faber, 1966.

Loy, Mina. *The Last Lunar Baedeker.* Edited by Roger L. Conover. Highlands: The Jargon Society, 1982.

———. *The Lost Lunar Baedeker.* Edited by Roger L. Conover. New York: Farrar, Straus and Giroux, 1996.

Moore, Marianne. *The Complete Poems of Marianne Moore.* New York: Macmillan/Penguin, 1994.

Pound, Ezra. *Selected Prose, 1909–1965.* Ed. William Cookson. New York: New Directions, 1973.

von Freytag-Loringhoven, Baroness Elsa. *Body Sweats: The Uncensored Writings of Elsa von Freytag-Loringhoven.* Eds. Irene Gammel and Suzanne Zelazo. Cambridge: MIT Press, 2011.

Acknowledgements

Earlier versions of some poems have appeared in print and online in *Jacket2* and *Dusie*, and in *Touch Donkey* #38 and *Poemeleon*. 'Citable Gestures' first appeared as a chapbook with derek beaulieu's no press (2017). An early version of that same poem (the epigraph of which is from a letter Pound wrote to Joyce in 1915), was part of a collaborative visual art piece by Dora Garcia exhibited at the Power Plant, Toronto (Dora Garcia: *I See Words, I Hear Voices*, September 2015–January 2016, curated by Chantal Pontbriand). The poem 'Tectonic Gaze' was written in response to Christian Bök's The Xenotext Book 1 and is included in the deluxe edition of that work (2015). The first line in 'Tectonic Gaze' is the opening line of H.D.'s poem 'Eurydice.'

Thanks to Alana Wilcox for so fearlessly charting the Canadian literary landscape, for her tireless efforts on behalf of writers, readers, and the word, and for her remarkable ability to ensure that every page sings. I am grateful to Jeramy Dodds for believing in this project, and for his invaluable contributions in shaping the manuscript. Both rob mclennan and derek beaulieu have been enormously supportive and I am most grateful for their efforts. I also want to thank Lizzie Gill for her astonishing collage on the cover of the book. I thank Roger Conover for the gift of Mina Loy and for finding the Baroness a home. Thank you to my soul-saving sisters Seana Zelazo, Janieta Eyre, and Patricia Olivier-Martin. For the conversations and lines of flight, I thank Christian Bök, Stephen Cain, David Dorenbaum, Nicky Drumbolis, Barry Near, and Priscila Uppal. To Phil Zelazo, thank you for never wavering. Thanks also to Andy Crosbie for his astounding ear and for always being there.

Suzanne Zelazo is a writer, editor, educator, and former professional triathlete who continues to coach cycling, running, and triathlon. She holds a PhD in English with a specialty in female modernism and avant-garde poetry and performance. She has worked in commercial sport publishing, founded and ran the small press literary magazine *Queen Street Quarterly*, and has taught literature and writing courses at York University and Ontario College of Art and Design University. Her scholarly publications include co-edited collections of writing by Baroness Elsa von Freytag-Loringhoven (MIT Press) and Florine Stettheimer (Book*hug). Her projects seek to integrate creative expression and the body.

Typeset in Walbaum and Transat

Printed at the Coach House on bpNichol Lane in Toronto, Ontario, on Zephyr Antique Laid paper, which was manufactured, acid-free, in Saint-Jérôme, Quebec, from second-growth forests. This book was printed with vegetable-based ink on a 1973 Heidelberg KORD offset litho press. Its pages were folded on a Baumfolder, gathered by hand, bound on a Sulby Auto-Minabinda, and trimmed on a Polar single-knife cutter.

Designed by Alana Wilcox
Cover image: *Crown Jewels* by Lizzie Gill
Author photo by Kristin Eff

Coach House Books
80 bpNichol Lane
Toronto ON M5S 3J4
Canada

416 979 2217
800 367 6360

mail@chbooks.com
www.chbooks.com